ANATOMIES

Dan Featherston

1998

Other books by Dan Featherston:

Rooms (Paper Brain Press)

26 Islands (primitive publications)

ANATOMIES

Dan Featherston

Potes & Poets Press
Elmwood CT
1998

For Melia

Potes & Poets Press *New* Chapbook Series #17

For further information about chapbooks in this series,
please write:

Potes & Poets Press
181 Edgemont Avenue
Elmwood CT 06110-1005

or email: potepoet@home.com

Objects Found in the Body

Si j'ai du goût, ce n'est guère
Que pour la terre et les pierres.

                -- Rimbaud

1. Stomach:

grape seeds, peas, peanuts, chocolate nuts, sprout-
ing beans, fruit stones, 122 robin-shot, 92 robin-
shot & 120 plum stones, a mass of straw, a stone, a
tooth, false teeth, a piece of horn, a rabbit's femur,
5 pounds 3 ounces of hair, several ounces of crude
mercury, a spoon, a rusty iron spoon 11 inches
long, 30 spoon handles, a fork, 2 iron forks, a
4-pronged fork, a knife, an earthen egg-cup, nee-
dles, pins, an iron pin, 2 pieces of rusty crooked
wire, nails, 9 cartwheel nails, 30 nails, 4 pounds of
old nails & a pair of compasses, 2 pairs of com-
passes, crushed glass, 6 screws, 10 ounces of
screws & bits of crockery, a piece of pipe, 15
medals of gold, 52 pieces of money, 100 louis

d'ors, a ring, buckles, a steel button-hook, a key, a
toothbrush, a swab 10 inches long, a pair of sus-
penders, 3 roller-bandages, 2 metal balls, a barrel
hoop, a brass pommel weighing 9 ounces, a de-
tached organ handle, the handle of a music-box, a
box containing dispatches from Napoleon, a rosary,
earth & holy medals.

2. Bladder:

a barley head, a sprig of wheat, hair, needles, pins,
hair-pins, a long wax taper, a pencil, a pencil-case,
a metallic sound, the handle of a toothbrush, 3
vertebrae of a squirrel, a hog's penis.

3. Rectum:

a button-hook, phosphorous matches, the frozen
tail of a pig, a bullock's horn measuring 11 inches,
a piece of wood measuring 7 inches, a stick 10
inches long, a long smooth stone, a mortar pestle, a

cylindrical snuff-box, a bottle of *l'eau de la reine de Hongrie*, a wine glass, a beer glass, a drinking goblet, a tin cup, a preserve-pot, a candle box.

4. Found in a Prisoner's Rectum:

a box of tools made of sheet iron, covered with skin, 6 inches long & 5 inches wide, weighing 22 ounces, containing a gun barrel 4 inches long, a mother-screw steel, a screw-driver, a saw of steel for cutting wood 4 inches long, another saw for cutting metal, a boring syringe, a prismatic file, a half-franc piece & 4 one-franc pieces tied together with thread, a piece of thread, a piece of tallow.

5. Vagina:

a ball of waxed string, a cotton reel, a silk-bobbin, a cedar pencil, a sponge, a drinking glass, a pewter cup, a small metallic pot, a live leech.

Pink

A pricked white like light dazzled chrome
bumper of blood idling at edge,
hint of sex in the fold:
eyelid, nipple, lip, pudenda.

Hint of *oeillet*, little French eye
shut up in pink's plosive
closed with a click.
Words see by their vowels.

A tinyness & term of endearment
possession diminishes,
shut red squinting through slip & slit.
Sails narrowly as Dutch vessel.
Swims in samlet & sliver-thin minnow.
Smallest finger.
Cheap red wine.
Maggot of the greenbottle fly.

A noise distributing its energy equally among the octaves.
More low frequency than white, less variance than red.

Not blue's somber hue.
Not purple's bruised red.
Chromatic alchemy
of innocence & experience:
pink clothes, pink toys, pink walls--
small buoyancies
while boys sail through
unobstructed, anchored in blue.

A doll aisle windowed with cellophane,
walled with pink cardboard.
Some sinister, sugar-coaxed thrill,
pink's trill.

Pink sash-pinched waist & ribboned hair.
Pink splash scattering red's lusty thrust of roses.

Pink shrimp, pink coral, pink cockatoo.
Elephant colored small--
red's bulk & broad blindness
stuffed through champagne eyelets.

Red wink under white austerity.
A hooded violence.
Pornography's smeared pink
a pure red & naughty white.
Pink politics leaning left,
seizing red sickle & hammer.

Pink stammers, blowing coy bubbles
from red mouths into white air.
Cream red. Ruddy white.
A pout. A stab.
Pink gin, pinkwash, pink wine, pink wood.
Thinks flamingo, carnation, plumeria.
Pink is your copy of the original.
Pink collared between white & blue.
Snooker pink ball & pink spot.

Brown pink, Dutch pink, French pink.

Pink's plink, metallic rattle.

Panties, bra & slip.

Lips stick too

some moral banter

between red & white.

Slip tinged pink touching her under.

An eye, a hole.

Hot pink's sass a brassy, brittle red.

Cool pink's whisper pricking white silence.

Odors

At Vetlianka all the plague patients diffused an odor of **honey.**

At Athens bees flew from a bull's entrails

& hornets from warlike horses.

In Egypt plagues swarmed out of the desert

like dark clouds & hovered over the cities.

In quarantine, hived away in cells.

*

Nursing infants
sour **butter**.

*

Scarlet fever
bread hot from the oven.

*

Menstruation distinguished by an odor of **leather**.
Saddled in blood, straddled abattoir of the body
turned inside out, hung to dry
between earth & sky.
Birth & death.
Hide: to turn "animal" inside out.

*

Suppressed menstruation
odor of **hops**
grain's combustion.

*

The Hungarian monk was able to decide
the chastity of females by smell alone.

*

The smell of fear

blood mingled with **electricity**.

*

The diabetic produces an odor of **apples**.

Breath's white-flowered branch

tinged brass like sunlight

caramelized in her skin.

*

In the paroxysms of hysteria & epilepsy

the hair's specific odor of **ozone**.

*

Hysterics will produce an odor of **violets**--

frenzied hue of bloomed earth,

sanitarium's guerdon

laced up in white jackets.

*

The sweat of lunatics resembles that of yellow **deer** or **mice**.
Scuttling between rooms, feverish in the wall.
Some glimpsed wilderness.

*

Measles: the smell of freshly plucked **feathers**.
Attributed to pillows
wet with fever
spotted skin pricked raw.

*

After sex the odor of **chloroform**
owing to a peculiar secretion
of the buccal glands.
A volatile, sweet taste
sluiced from loosed limbs.

*

Orteschi met a young lady who exhaled
the strong odor of **vanilla**
from the joints of her fingers.

*

The syphilitic produces an odor of stagnant **water**
as if the sexual turbine
turned in upon
itself.

*

The odor of typhoid
that of **blood**.

*

Chorea produces an odor of **pineapple**.

St. Vitus never tasted a pineapple

but might have thought of the dance

as a kind of torrid sweetness

under the tough exterior of Roman law.

*

Lethargy & catalepsy produce a **cadaverous** odor.

Some people have a cadaverous odor

their whole life.

A prophecy.

A hint.

The Hand

*The object that first visually disappears in an infant's play
with worldly objects is the inside of its own hand...*

   — Maxine Sheets-Johnstone, *The Roots of Thinking*

1.

There are languages in the hand

Latin bones & German blood.

There is romance in the hand,

but the bones are broken.

What broke the bones inside the hand?

Was there a time when the hand was whole?

The wrist is the neck of the arm.

Desire turned the wrist

& broke the bone

to make a face in the palm.

2.

Hand's *hinthan* is to take.

What has the hand taken?

What has it given?

There is a drawing of a hand in the book

held together with words:

Scaphoid	boat
Magnum	great
Trapezoides	trapezoid
Trapezium	table
Lunate	moon
Cuneiform	wedge
Pisiform	pea
Unciform	hook

A man sits in a boat at a great, trapezoidal table under the moon.

On the table there is a wedge, a pea & a hook.

How will he handle these things?

His voice is a hand:

There are shapes buried in the hand--

a triangle, a circle & a semi-circle

inside a trapezoid inside a scaphoid under a circle.

There is a name for each shape buried in the hand,

each thing handled by its name inside the hand.

I am named by what I see,

seated before a wedge, a pea & a hook

at a great, trapezoidal table in a boat under the moon.

3.

What loosed the webbing & shattered the hoof?

What hardened the wing?

Distance.

What is the distance between the hand & the fin?

The distance between air & water.

What is the distance between the hand & the hoof?

The distance between air & earth.

What is the distance between the hand & the wing?

The distance between air & air.

4.

Something like water has shaped your hands.

Before you were born your hands

were the first things you held.

You would curl them close to your body

as if to disappear through the hole in holding.

5.

We admired the ice sculpture of the fish

disappearing behind a mesh of weeds.

When fish & weeds rounded off,

polished by the heat,

we were reminded of time,

as if a clock of ice

turned backward toward a memory of water.

6.

Your wrists swivel like fins.

Your fingers move like feathers.

Your palms curl in like hooves.

To say you in fin, feather & hoof--

not true or untrue

but these amplitudes

both of & beyond you.

7.

Was it reaching for something over & over that broke our hands?

Is it the memory of water our wrists trace like rivulets,

moving upright over the savannah's primal ocean?

What rain has fallen over our hands for millennia?

What forced the thumb's slow migration away from the fingers?

Our hands bear the shape of fear & survival:

miracle of the wrist;

miracle of the thumb, that hominid flag!

8.

There is catastrophe in the hand. There are hands that
break the world & hands broken by the world. There are
hands crushed in conveyors & mangled in doors. There
are fingers whipped by the bandsaw & bruised by the

ruler. I ask you what is meant by the gangster holding his handgun parallel to the earth, aimed at another man's head. "It means his life's hardly worth the effort of taking aim." The way animals are put down.

9.

There are phantom hands & the one thousand hands of the gods. There are shadows in the hand. The puppet's life is a hand. There are hands cradling invisible babies & pounding invisible walls. There are hands adjusting imaginary crowns. There are hands bleeding stigmata. There is ink & splintered wood in the hand. There are hands sticking up out of rubble & empty hands held up to the sky after the disaster. There are hands beckoning from graves, passing through walls, signaling behind fire & glass.

10.

At the virtual reality lab, I slip my hand into a glove
with fiber-optic spines running along each finger.
Peering into a visor, I reach for the virtual door-
knob & feel it nuzzle in my palm, brain dizzy in
that alchemy of eye & hand.

11.

In the hand, space breaks into pieces. In the hand,
time breaks into pieces. You say, "Look how the
hawk turns, tilting against a table of wind." What
eddies of space pool round our hands that they
wince like eyes, pivot like wings? What do the
hands see? Wind, heat & fear, voices, a flaw in the
fabric. Touching you, my hands are eyes.

12.

The hand is ancestor of machines, measures &
numbers. We leave our prints in the name of the
hand placed upon objects. Handmill's "mill moved
by the hand". The hands of armchairs disappear

into wilderness, curled under in a lion's paw, falcon's talon. Like a corpse, a chair has legs, arms, back & seat, but no face. There is sadness in a room full of empty chairs. In chairs we face civility seated inside animals & skeletons. We sit down inside a mask turned backward & peer out from its hollow.

13.

Your hands reach upward like birds tethered to your wrists. Your hands fold inward like sleeping animals. When you thread a needle or twirl a fork, when you hold a pen or sprinkle salt, the whole world sifts between your fingers-- trellising chains of matter, leafy mosaics, braids of sand & sea, starry turbans, diaphanous weeds.

14.

Drawn to neurological scale the hands are giants dwarfing head, genitals, trunk & legs. Time & space multiply in the hand, unfolding like imbricate

buds. There are alphabets & numbers in the hand.
There are maps & diamond mines & faces in the
hand. There are horns & wings & tools in the hand.
There are bridges & barbwire & steeples in the
hand. There are people in the hand. There are
cocks & cunts in the hand. There are nightsticks,
pistols & handcuffs in the hand. There are eyes &
anger & prayer in the hand. There are doorways &
windows in the hand. There is a gang of five in the
hand. There is a flower & a rock in the hand.
There is a table in the hand.

15.

Your hidden hand is a bouquet or a knife. A salve,
a poison. Empty, they are full of history. Is the
hand jealous of the world? The hand's distance
pinches mountains, props leaning towers. The
astronaut's thumb snuffs out the world. The finger
on the button destroys the world outside the hand &
the hand inside the world. There is a closed book
of anger inside the fist. There is an open book of

giving in the palm. The hand is a book whose words are deeds.

16.

The palm is the face of the hand. It is a map of love's country, fortune's country, life's country. There are mountains & planets in the palm. There is a book of birth & death folded in the palm.

17.

Hand listening to a lover's body mute under clothing. Hand parting jungle vines. Scarred hand, hennaed hand, ringed & braceleted hand. Hands asleep in pockets. An admiral's hands held behind his back. A child's hands opening toward mother, toward other. There is a wave breaking in the hand signaling toward land. The first hand waves the world in trailed by a wake of ink. The last hand waves the world away trailed by a wake of silence.

Soap

The size of a deck of cards,

a shirt pocket,

a pack of cigarettes,

a transistor radio.

Weight of a small bird or a hand.

*

Saddle. Crescent. Oval. Lozenge. Rectangle.

Match the shape to the hand.

Match the shape to the hand in the mind.

Gritty soap flecked with pumice & oat.

Smooth soap like polished marble.

Opaque soap. Translucent soap.

The colorless, odorless soap of public washrooms.

The bright, perfumed soap of private baths.

The soap sliver, cracked & flaking,

too small to hold & thrown away.

*

The marketer of soap considers
the marriage of soap & hands:
wrapped in colored paper
& tied with bright ribbons;
wrapped in rough, simple paper;
wrapped in clear cellophane.

Odor

What is the odor of cleanliness?
rose, jasmine, coconut, almond,
oatmeal, talc, amber, sandalwood.

*

Cleanliness: something fit perfectly to the palm.
Carved wood, a gold bullion.

Of color

Clean colors of soap: ivory, powder blue, lemon, grass.
Light greens, soft blues, weak whites, pink, reds & violets.

Beautiful objects small

If there is a ribbon, untie it. Slide a finger
under the wrapper. Feel the glue give.
Slide your finger along the fold.
Opens like a palm, a curled leaf, a shell.
Perfume wafts up. Blue soap streaked white
a piece of sky fit in the palm,
as if clean hands were windows.

Smoothness

A cake of soap, *a slope of earth, polished surfaces . . .*

Memory slides like oil over the world. Palpable & elusive.
Hard to hold in the white amnesia of porcelain.

Cleanliness: forgetfulness?

The baptism, the abdest, the lachrymal, Lethe.

The color of water. The color of no-birth, no-death.

*

Tears: a kind of lubricant oiling the friction

between the eye & what it sees.

What do the eyes see?

An inward sense of melting & languor.

Beauty acts by relaxing the solids of the whole system.

Is there beauty in forgetting?

A roundness, smoothness & weak cohesion of the parts.

Water & oil, the vehicles of all taste.

Tears-- a way of tasting?

Insipid, inodorous, colorless, smooth.

*

The smooth of taste, the beautiful of taste. Smooth globular bodies, as the marbles with which boys amuse themselves, rolled backward & forward & over one another. There is a species of motion which relaxes more than rest; a gentle oscillatory motion, a rising & falling. Rocking sets children to sleep better than absolute rest.

Oiling the gears of sleep, what wakefulness would tears wash away? What does taste remember? Cleaning his hands was a kind of sleep. How the skin forgets the world.

*

Is there nostalgia in soap? Is there nostalgia for the feel of things shaped by the hand? The engineer of soap considers the psychology of cleanliness. Puritan soap. Colonial soap. Soap cut roughly by a machine to imitate a penknife's whittling.

The effect of words

The insignia on the wrapper:

gold spray over gold letters.

The king's hands cleansed by gold.

Everything he touches made clean.

Gold. The wealth in cleanliness.

A rare earth of regal stones

smooth & oily to the touch like tears.

*

Soap cakes stamped like gold bullion, bricks.

Dial to ring clear.

Dove postdiluvial.

Irish Springs forth all things green.

Coast is clear. To glide effortlessly,

far from dingy taverns & towns.

*

They washed his mouth with soap for saying unclean words.

They held his head back

& scrubbed the dirty words out of his tongue.

It tasted bitter because of the words.

How will they clean the mind's dirty hand,

the mind made dirty handling words?

The mind is a dirty hole.

Daub your finger with soap.

Put it into the holes where dirt grows:

before the tongue & behind the ears,

before the meal & after the crime,

before the mass & after the confession,

at the doorways of bathrooms,

churches & operating rooms.

At the doorway of a word,

Wash thyself of thy hands.

The doors themselves cleanse.

No fingerprints on the soap.

A kind of glove.

A doorknob.

A cleansing silence.

The artificial infinite

The soap is a mirror unstained by looking & touching.

You turn the soap between your palms

& the edges shape to your hands,

smooth like lathed wood.

You work from the outside in,

drawing dirt from the inside out.

A man soaping his body comes clean of conscience.

No blame. Even the soap is clean

like the dream of a perfect crime,

a hand that touches without touching.

*

Her fingernails press tiny moons into the soap.

He sees bodies deciphered in the soft tablet's
cursive script. The child imagines animals
jettisoned from between his legs,
nosing forward blindly under soapy
islands afloat in polar seascapes.

*

The dish shaped like a seashell.
The soap a grain of dirt
hands turn to pearl.

The philosophy of soap

Cleanliness is a perfect crime.
No fingerprints.
No evidence.

The soap like a door between dirty & clean.
The soap turned open in his hands.
The soap that is the opposite of his hands.

How does one hand clean the other?

He washed his hands, then dirtied them on the doorknob.

He dirtied his hands on the doorknob, then washed them.

How will you leave this room with clean hands?

How do you clean soap?

The beautiful in feeling

Observe the parts of a woman where she is perhaps the most beautiful, about the neck & breasts; the smoothness; the softness; the easy swell; the variety of the surface, which is never for the smallest space the same; the maze through which the unsteady eye slides giddily, without knowing where to fix or whither it is carried.

Soaping your body, tracing your thigh, leg up on the smooth basin, toes curled round, ropes of soapy water dripping from your cunt hair, lathering your belly, breasts smooth, slippery with soap.

Cleansed: would mean for you to disappear? You are a window I clean with my hands. The window of your body lovely to look through? to look at? Or is it how we each endure within ourselves -- the resistance of your body against my hand, the resistance of my hand against your body -- that I would trace & retrace, *pleasant by the slightest resistance along the surface or to the presence of the parts on one another.*

Are our bodies clean or dirty? Is it my own hand that is unclean? Or is it this resistance we would cleanse -- this distance -- bringing you close, sliding against you, this suspension touching cleanses.

Sources

Objects Found in the Body, Odors: source material found in George Gould's *Anomalies & Curiosities of Medicine.*

Soap: interpolated passages from Edmund Burke's *A Philosophical Enquiry into the Origin of our Ideas of the Sublime and Beautiful.*